God Made Me! Who Am I?

Jungle Animals

SONCOAST PUBLISHING

written
and illustrated
by
Sally Blass Murray

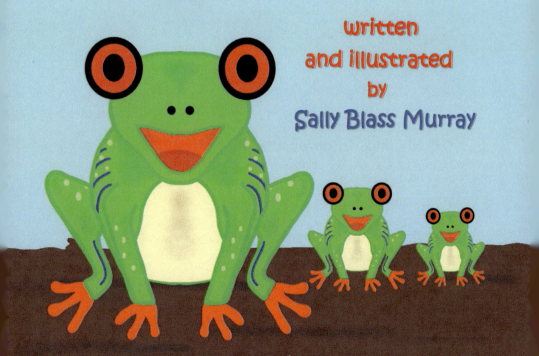

God Made Me! Who Am I?

Copyright © 2021 Sally Blass Murray
ISBN 978-1-953406-35-4

All rights reserved

Author photo by Kathy Bell kbellaphotography

Published by Soncoast Publishing
P.O. Box 1503
Hartselle, AL 35640
www.soncoastpublishing.com

Scripture quotations have been taken from the Christian Standard Bible®, Copyright © 2017 by Holman Bible Publishers. Used by permission. Christian Standard Bible® and CSB® are federally registered trademarks of Holman Bible Publishers.

Printed in the United States of America

From the author –

I praise the Lord every day as I write.
He gives me words and a call
to help little hearts know more about Him...
THE Author, Creator of ALL.

Note to Parents, Grandparents, Teachers

This series of books was designed to provide a fun, lighthearted, interactive experience between parents (grandparents/teachers) and their young children, while honoring God as our Creator.

The teacher in me hopes that it will also be a learning experience, so each poem is based on a fact (or several facts) about each creature. To that end, you may want to suggest that children wait until you ask, "Who am I?" before they give an answer. This will ensure that they hear all the clues and possibly learn some new facts! Also, I purposely used some words that your young child may not yet know, so that you can talk with your little one about their meanings. They will love this interaction with you!

Lastly, as you read to your child, I pray that you will be able to have deeper conversations about Jesus and the fact that God gave His only Son for us! My heart's desire is that your child will come to know Christ and will use their talents to praise Him in their own unique ways!

*With a grateful heart
and my deepest thanks
to*

Jesus

my **Savior**
my **Lord**
my **Dearest Friend**

*"Let everything that breathes
praise the Lord.
Hallelujah!"*

Psalms 150:6
CSB

About the Author

Sally Blass Murray is a mother, grandmother, and retired elementary school music teacher with degrees in Church Music and Music Education. She has always loved music, rhyme, rhythm, and playing with words. Sally loves to write and has a passion for sharing the love of God with children through her books.

She believes that all of us have God-given gifts and that we should use them to encourage others and bring honor to Christ.

This book is part of a series of "God Made Me! Who Am I?" books.

Titles include:

God Made Me! Who Am I?
Jungle Animals

God Made Me! Who Am I?
Insects

God Made Me! Who Am I?
Zoo Animals

God Made Me! Who Am I?
Ocean Creatures

God Made Me! Who Am I?
Farm Animals

**Available at Soncoastpublishing.com
and
Amazon.com**

I praise the Lord
for my size and my strength.

I can grow to weigh
six hundred pounds!

My beautiful coat
is striped orange and black

and my ROAR
makes a VERY loud sound!

God made me!

Who am I?

Tiger

God made tigers and...

I praise the Lord
for my really huge snout!

My sense of smell is quite keen!

I do not have teeth,
but my tongue's like a spoon...

it scoops up my "insect cuisine!"

God made me!

Who am I?

Anteater

God made tigers, anteaters, and...

I praise the Lord
for my glorious stripes!

My mane is spectacular too!

When thinking of words
that start with a "Z" ...

My name will be helpful to you!

God made me!

Who am I?

Zebra

God made tigers, anteaters, zebras, and...

I praise the Lord
for my shaggy, red fur!

I spend most of my time in a tree.

My arms are SO strong,
if I swing from a vine,

I can carry my baby with me!

God made me!

Who am I?

Orangutan

God made tigers, anteaters, zebras, orangutans, and...

I praise the Lord
for my cool, shedding skin!

My patterns identify me.

I slither around,
so watch where you step...

It's best if you just "let me be!"

God made me!

Who am I?

Snake

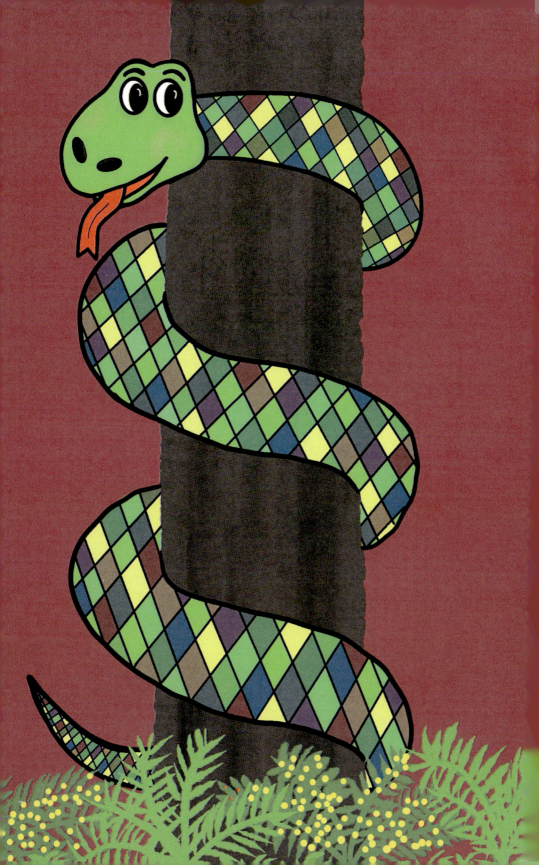

God made tigers, anteaters, zebras, orangutans, snakes, and...

I praise the Lord
for my bright-colored bill!

The sounds that I make
are SO funny!

Although I'm a bird,
I don't fly very well...

In the treetops,
I hop like a bunny!

God made me!

Who am I?

Toucan

God made tigers, anteaters, zebras, orangutans, snakes, toucans, and...

I praise the Lord
for how quickly I run!

On land, I'm the fastest, they say!

I purr like a cat
and have beautiful spots

that camouflage me night and day!

God made me!

Who am I?

Cheetah

God made tigers, anteaters, zebras, orangutans, snakes, toucans, cheetahs, and...

I praise the Lord
for my big, toothy grin!

My jaws are powerful, too!

My back's very "spikey"
and so is my tail...

I'm a little bit scary,
it's true!

God made me!

Who am I?

Crocodile

God made tigers, anteaters, zebras, orangutans, snakes, toucans, cheetahs, crocodiles, and...

We praise the Lord
in our own unique ways.

God made us special, you see?

We are all different
and that's really great...

There's no one like you or like me!

God made us!

Who are we?

People